Amazing Eggs

Contents

What is an egg?

duck eggs

An egg is where an animal begins its life.

butterfly eggs

frog eggs

Eggs can look very different.
Some eggs have a shell around
them. Others have a sort of jelly.

Which animals lay eggs?

fish

toad

Many animals lay eggs. Some animals lay eggs in water.

snake

ant

ostrich

Others lay eggs on land.

Where do animals lay their eggs?

A weaverbird weaves a nest out of long grass stems.

Many animals make a nest for their eggs.

A stickleback makes a nest with plants.

Animals make their nests from materials they find around them.

How do animals look after their eggs?

A penguin warms his egg on his feet.

Animals look after their eggs in different ways.

An earwig cleans her nest.

A crocodile guards her nest.

Why do animals hide their eggs?

A turtle hides her eggs in the sand.

Some animals hide their eggs.
This keeps the eggs safe from
other animals.

Can you see these bird eggs?

Some eggs are camouflaged.
This makes them harder to see.

What is inside an egg?

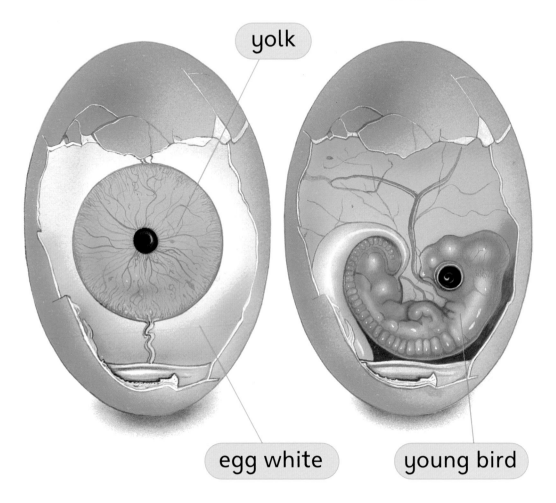

yolk

egg white

young bird

A bird is growing inside this egg.
It feeds on the yolk and the watery
egg white.

shell

young bird

Every day the bird grows a little bit bigger.

How does an egg hatch?

A tortoise egg hatches after about
ten weeks. The young tortoise chips
a little hole in the shell with a
special tooth.

It uses its legs and feet to break the shell open. The young tortoise crawls out!

a
b
c
d
e
f
g
h
i
j
k
l
m
n
o
p
q
r
s
t
u
v
w
x
y
z

Index